Spirituality
In
HEALING
And
LIFE

Brian R. Clement

Foreword by Marilyn Diamond

Cover and Book Design
by Joyce Murray

Library of Congress Cataloging-In-Publication Data

Clement, Brian R. 1997
    Spirituality in Healing and Life

    ISBN 0-9622373 $7.95
    1. Philosophy. 2. Health. 3. Mind and Body.

Copyright 1997 by Brian R. Clement

Cover and book design by Joyce Murray

Printed in the United States of America

DEDICATION

To the heart and soul
of the six billion of us.

"We must put theology into the action of real life."

CONTENTS

FOREWARD

There was a time when I believed that the key to healthy living was entirely dependent upon a perfectly healthy diet, consumed religiously-- all of the time. Like so many others, I had confused physical wellness with total health. During those years, my level of health rose and fell, despite impressive physical efforts, as a result of lack of nourishment on a soul level. I found my way to prayer and meditation and mental detoxification strategies, and I began to recognize a delightful balance of body fitness, mental stability and spiritual clarity. That state, in my opinion, is the true health we are all capable of experiencing.

Fortunately, in this era there is a movement towards 'well being', in which our goal of health on the physical level is not separate from our longing for wellness on the spiritual level. Complete health is much more complex and profound than just taking care of the body. The key ingredient to living a healthy life is learning to be happy. And the one factor which secures true happiness is spiritual awareness and practice.

Having observed the talented guidance offered to the visitors at Hippocrates firsthand, I am pleased to see Brian Clement's integration of effective food therapies and spiritual support. The psychological and emotional therapy that is encouraged during the physical cleansing process is transformative. It empties the physical body of blocks to make space for inner growth--spiritual evolution. Brian has been an inspiration to many thousands of people who have turned to him in the most fearful, vulnerable moments of their lives. One person at a time, he seeks to replace despair and hopelessness with health and renewal of spirit. Clearly, he has profound insight into the technology and psychology of healing on all levels.

Embracing a spiritual path will direct you through the rocky times, but, more importantly, will be your inspiration as you maneuver your way through life. Know that you are connected to that tangible, inner world which cannot be seen, heard, tasted, or smelled, but *can* be felt. Realize and embrace your true nature and relationship with God. This alone will empower you to consciously create your own destiny, to overcome life's obstacles with grace, and to manifest your dreams.

Marilyn Diamond

INTRODUCTION

Over the last several decades at Hippocrates Health Institute, we have discovered a consistent and evident pattern in human life and healing: There is no true life or health that does not include spirituality.

The workings of anatomy and physiology and the effects that emotions have on you are quite blatant, and for the most part well understood. Elusiveness prevails when we reach the spiritual ingredient due to the abstract and disconnected way that we perceive it. It has been my observation that this lack of stability within the spiritual process comes from our inability to accept anything that is not based on atoms, molecules and structure.

Intellect, with all of its ritualistic and systematic trappings, is generally the first approach to a spiritual life. But only an open consciousness, not intellectual formulas has the potential to permit the freedom of spirit.

In this writing it is my objective to clarify and make accessible the process known as "spiritual thought."

This knowledge has come to me through working with thousands of people who are embracing enormous change and reaching out for grand accomplishments. Their spirit is the pinnacle ingredient in their evolving life. From those who have healed themselves from catastrophic disease to those who have taken an ordinary, acceptable life and molded it into a happy life- the enormity of spirit is a constant in the process.

Too often the unseen is easy to forget. We are about to show you that that which you cannot touch, feel or taste is the greatest nourishment of all.

Chapter One
DEFINING SPIRITUALITY

Spirituality and religion are synonymous thoughts within humanity today. It has been my observation and experience that religion has given a format and a goal for people to comprehend and apply the principles and practices of religion's teachings. However, we often find ourselves caught in a mechanical response to the principles and rituals, which prevents a spiritual experience. People can achieve the desired consciousness from systematic teaching when they truly understand that the written word is dead and only the *application* of that thought is viable. Religion can be a great assistance in elevating individual and universal understandings, yet sadly, throughout history we have watched people manipulate great teachings and eradicate any spirit that dwelled within them.

***

Recently, I was conducting a lecture and when the time for "Questions and Answers" came, a strong, young man who was a pilot stood and challenged a statement that I had made. My statement was quite definite and given without hesitation: "There is no true life or health that does not include spirituality." He asked why I would even propose such a thing, thinking from his own experience that what I was saying was that one must be committed to a set of dogmatic teachings to have a full life. In explaining my belief, I suggested that he imagine for a moment a simple circumstance: "You are driving home tonight and a slow-moving car driven by an older person is coming down the same road you are about to turn in to. If you choose to wait so that the other driver will not be startled...that would be a spiritual act."

We must put theology into the action of real life. Our spirit needs continual usage to empower us with the profound potential of human experience. Within each of our souls we have the ability to sensitize ourselves to all that exists. By doing so, we will vigorously raise our integrity so that from the heart to the environment, we are creating a spiritual experience. Our environment may then return this favor to us as long as we are willing to allow this level of freedom into our hearts. We are given endless opportunities for enjoying the spirit through every thought and action that we permit. The understanding that all involvement is as spiritual as it is physical and emotional can bring a feeling of relief, or a burden beyond comprehension. Relief prevails when you truly see how the wisdom of the heart gives you complete reign over all that occurs. It is perceived as a burden, when the mind believes that it alone has responsiblity for creating a good life.

***

I remember years ago, a lady with a serious illness who came to Hippocrates. During a consultation with me, she discussed the forty-nine years and six months of her life. Her eyes sparkled, her words elevated both of our spirits as she talked about how priviledged and secure she felt that her parents, her husband, and her children were all her best friends. Together they had created the many successes that she knew as life. At the end of this eulogy of happiness, she took a deep breath, then began to sob as the next words blurted out"...and then six months ago my doctor gave me six months to live!"

For the first time in my decades of work, I saw with clarity how most of us view our problems. I asked her: "Is who you are the fortynine and a half years of success or the six months of disease?" She stopped sobbing and after a moment of deep thought said: "Of course, my full and happy life." Today, years later, this lady has not only fully recovered, she is flourishing beyond her highest goals.

***

Our acceptance of problems as 'reality' and successes as 'luck' is the greatest preventer of true spirituality. When people have elevated themselves to a place of fulfilled contentment, they will not permit the strife of non-awareness to eat them alive. Within each of our worlds there is a constant higher place. Our only deterrent from living with this is our own inability to accept unconditional love.

***

We can get stuck in a merry-go-round of history. With the world moving more rapidly each day, individual security is melting like ice in August. This expeditious phenomenon is our starting point to move forward into an existence without pain and suffering, further, without disease and disorder, and ultimately, with happiness every minute of life. Is this not the essence that each of us truly desires? Only the most avid intellectual would have difficulty accepting this deep within themselves.

There are countless ways to reach this state of happiness. Reaching it is not difficult. But one must muster the courage to leave behind all pre-conceived ideas which encourage limitation and boundaries. Can we go beyond a set of rules, and allow the living force of spirituality to govern our

"Muster the courage
to leave behind
all preconceived ideas
which encourage limitation
and boundaries."

very existence? Granted our largest excuse is that worldly practices and daily routines call us back from this place of consciousness to a less aware level. Challenge yourself to the possibility that these everyday activities also contain a higher purpose. When people see their jobs, obligations and matter-of-fact acts as important as a time in prayer, they will capture the full warmth of living spiritually.

***

Not too long ago while I was exercising at a gymnasium, a friend I'm always pleased to meet revealed that he had spent several years in a concentration camp during the second world war. He was certainly atypical, with his abundance of positive thought and enormous charismatic spirit, always "up", always smiling, truly happy. My own encounters with survivors had etched an image in my mind of a hurt and often deeply sad individual that demonstrated what human cruelty and a persecutor's lack of spirit could do. Puzzled by the contrast, I asked my friend how he managed to have such a joyous life. His answer was pure, honest and correct when he said: "If I accepted any less, my persecutor would have achieved his goal."

***

"Wisdom is not taught or learned. It permeates true consciousness."

In spite of the physical and emotional things that may be occuring, we know from the heart of consciousness that we can capture happiness and gain from embracing the spirit. Transforming your life is not about safety. It is surely about courage. Each thought that we transform into action will give us an opportunity to find joy in our pursuits. When asking yourself why you're doing something, question further if your true desire is to gain happiness from it.

***.

Young children are the best representatives of human possibility. Free-thinking, limitless, authentic openness governs their every act until they slowly incorporate the ritualistic thoughts from their elders. We have often been told that we become wiser as time passes. Yet, is it not that we become more conditioned and mold ourselves into a smoother and more acceptable member of society? Wisdom is not taught or learned. It permeates true consciousness and is ever-present for us to utilize. Fortunately, we cannot control or manipulate wisdom as so many in the past have tried to do. This is why children who use the tool of instinct with their lack of experience can move forward without fear. We, as maturing individuals, are restrained from instinct and wisdom due to

*"Limited perception
can limit your life."*

the ever-haunting influence of intellect. How often have you found yourself analyzing whether you should move forward as an opportunity flies away? While the child would not only be seated on the flight, he may even be piloting the plane.

Sometimes this level of open understanding is assessed as a dangerous and overly simple theory in human awareness. But there is no reason that we should evaluate such clarity as negative. It is for us to develop passion which enlarges promise. This boundless arena of expansive spirituality is the real remedy for an unhappy life.

***

There are many dimensions within a single thought. This is a matter of perception. Two people can be involved in the same occurrence and evaluate the experience in different ways. For instance, when one is playing a sport, they conclude that this act is a physical enhancement, whereas the person sitting in the bleachers may feel it to be inspirational. How often are you aware of which areas or dimensions you are now pursuing? Limited perception can limit your life.

***

One of the most interesting events I have ever witnessed was a spiritual-healing gathering at a large Catholic cathedral. People came from all corners of the globe to meet the frail, young father with the quiet voice. There was none of the inspirational singing or fiery demonstration from this soulful spirit, but as people came to see him there was often one who left their wheelchair or dropped their cane. Outwardly, it appeared that the priest was physically healing people, but in terms of spirit, what was occurring was that some of the reciprocants were letting go of the physical and emotional anchors and embracing an expanded awareness. Yet today, I see too many people still searching for the healer rather than utilizing the wisdom of their hearts.

***

People close to me have devoted their entire lives to spiritual practice. Without hesitation I will say that they are contributing to a heightening of life. But I have conjectured that they would be assisting this process even more if they joined society and supported all the faithful, rather than try to persuade others to participate in their own perception.

Years ago, while lecturing in Jerusalem I had spent time with one of the high Rabbis who explained that there was nothing mystical in life, there was only the inability for us to see something as possible. In spite of all the difficulties which pervade the holy part of life, we are individually capable of fulfilling our own dreams. When truly searching for your place, do not wander beyond the room that houses fulfillment.

***

As Ghandi and Martin Luther King demonstrated, personal elevation engages global change. Each drop of goodness that you create will bring your spirit to a more usable level. Using the spirit is the essence of our existence. We come from the invisible as a spark of life, and we leave to the invisible once again. Through understanding the enormity of this very thought, we may gather enough faith to let go of who we think we are and BE who we really are. This is difficult in a world of illusion which is based on what we see, touch, feel and taste. Our significance on a physical level is no more than a gathering of endless electrons. How dare we make ourselves into concrete! An endless stream of invisible life flows like the greatest waterfall for us to bathe in, and we still stand on the shore, dry as a bone.

***

Be kind to yourself so that all your encounters will be enriched by your own possibility. Do not wait for mighty acts and far away saviours to participate in who you are. There are no walls

"We come from
the invisible,
as a spark of life,
and we leave
to the invisible
once again."

that you cannot walk through, or worlds that you cannot reach.

***

Are you feeling the profound importance of self-elevation at this moment? If you are still experiencing just words on paper, go get a recording of Bach's baroque music. Turn it up as loud as is comfortable. Close all the doors. Shut your eyes. Slowly and freely move around letting the music quiet your mind and fill you heart. Or, take yourself to a beach at dawn, and in the quiet, walk alone until the full sun warms your skin. Find a place in the center of a forest and sit in peace, observing, feeling, and allowing all to occur. These are but a few ways of capturing where you should be all of the time. In the middle of a day of busy work, your heart should feel that it is bathing in the light of God.

These feelings are often so foreign to us that we find ways to denounce them. Individually hundreds of millions of us have created negative personas through our own pain, and cannot validate the pleasure of the spirit as anything more than illusion.

In modern times the quest for spiritual life is often misguided. We search for structure and once again become entrapped in the practice of

"As we move forward,
it is our obligation to
expand our limited
faith and to gather true
strength from the very
act of surrender."

theology. For each and every one of the billions of people that reside on this incredible planet, our spirituality is personal. It can be reached through the better known ways as long as you perceive them as just a springboard, not as a foundation. God has endless ability, and most of us are still struggling with a fraction of 1% of the 100% that is possible.

Our own arrogance permits us to believe that we know enough to put words in the mouth of God when in all earnestness there are no words necessary. Reaching into your soul will do more for you than searching outside of your awareness.

***

Without hesitation you should strive for blind faith. This is the only true faith that does not demand proof on physically based occurences. We practice blind faith many times in our life without acknowledging it. For instance, if you have ever fully loved someone, you trusted your feelings completely, and although you have physically never seen love, did you not absolutely believe in it, and want more of it?

As we move forward, it is our obligation to expand our limited faith and to gather true strength from the very act of surrender.

***

**Spirituality
is not only achievable, it is your
birthright. Be humble enough,
brave enough and secure enough
to utilize it with every breath.**

Chapter two
UTILIZING SPIRITUALITY

Utilizing spiritual thought is more important than understanding spirituality. Our own concept of spirituality creates boundaries and permits us to feel falsely conscious. Without complete understanding one is still able to proceed with action. Too often we force our lives into a narrow and dark place through our reluctance to act.

***

Many years ago at a large gathering thousands of people began running in my direction. Without thought I joined the group as they rushed by and proceeded to feel the unified energy. It may have been four or five minutes before I bothered to ask "What are we doing?" Interestingly enough, the people who surrounded me all expressed the same question. On a mental level this was certainly absurd and had no significance that was practical. On the spiritual level it was embracing, exciting, fulfilling and joyous. Isn't it interesting how we try to determine what is right and wrong through social acceptance?

***

Throughout history many of our concepts have undergone continual changes. For example, an international periodical recently wrote about heaven and gave an historic outline of how we have perceived it over several centuries. They visited the Judeo-Christian concept which seems to recreate itself about every 50 - 75 years, and led us to now, the beginning of a new millenium, pointing out that many of the established religions today shy away from discussing heaven other than at funerals. Many of our great theologians have discounted the "pearly gates" for a more practical place that is nondescript. In this short voyage, looking at just one aspect of acceptable spiritual history, we see its endless transformation depending on the needs of the current culture. Isn't it interesting that even the great foundations of thought from your spiritual past can dissolve into fluidity and still be relevant?

***

I suggest that you review your present thoughts on all things spiritual by writing them down, and every sixty days reviewing, adding and subtracting to the original. Most of the time you will see a growing understanding, which permits you to open new doors of contentment. From this simple and revealing effort you will unveil the

the obvious. As you increase your spirituality, your life will be one of greater happiness. By allowing yourself to limit your growth more problems will surface.

Hopefully, this will compel you to acknowledge the paramount significance that spirituality plays in your life. We must take our thoughts and nurture them, permitting a burgeoning flood of consciousness to pervade our lives. Our growth in spirituality will bring us to places of greatness.

***

We often create heroes and dream of being like them some day. Understand that what you like in others is what is possible for you. We are all equals without question. Our only difference is our active participation in faith.

***

Recently, when I was conducting a course at Hippocrates, I spoke about the importance of faith in the process of healing, strongly stating that you must give away your pre-conditioned notion that something must be proven before you are willing to embrace faith. When the course ended, a devoutly religious woman quietly said that she totally disagreed about faith not needing motivation. She went on to say that "God will

"We must take our thoughts and nurture them, permitting a burdgeoning flood of consciousness to pervade our lives."

certainly give us signs so that we know we are on the right track." Understanding why she felt like this I did not try to dispute her. I let a moment pass and then proposed that the thing that differentiates humans from all other life as we know it is a free will. Further, I suggested that free will was the greatest gift given to us, but as in the first page of every owner's manual the instructions clearly state: "When using this equipment, one must be totally responsible."

Responsibility in our hands does not demand that the Higher Powers spend all of their time guiding us. Within our very thoughts we are given a roadmap to success. This success will only come to fruition through the incredible integrity-rich actions that we generate. Applying spirit to everything we do will assure us the freedom of an expansive life. Love will surface as a lightpost on our route to eternity. We feel it deep in our souls, and in the finest moments of our lives. But to capture it in a more permanent way you must permit yourself to accept Blind Faith.

How many of us have the ability to let go of the norms and freely say what we feel, do what we love and love what we do? If you even hesitate when asked this question, your obligation to work harder on your path to happiness is evident. Ask

Success comes from the integrity-rich actions we generate.

yourself if the abundance of good is too much for you to bear -- or the abundance of negativity is too much for you to bear? Put yourself in a place of total honesty and there is no question that your acts will be genuine. Give yourself half-truths and your life will be a half-life. "What's in it for me?" is the constant cry from humanity today. We must take this whining verbiage and elevate it to a melodic statement of "There is nothing that is not possible!"

***

I once heard someone interview a survivor of drowning: a man who had actually been trapped under an ice-cold Canadian lake for two hours. It was a remarkable event because up until then science had established that after six minutes being immersed in similar conditions, the body functions would die. And here sat someone who proved that this was not true. When asked what his experience was like, he explained that he "went to a place of comfort" before he was abruptly called back to life. His remembered experience was diversely opposite the physical trauma of cold and wet that he had suffered. Perhaps this is a message each of us can learn from. However horrific we perceive a situation

"Applying spirit to everything we do will assure us the freedom of an expansive life."

to be, we should work hard to get to its opposite, where light and goodness reign.

"Goodness" can be subjected to millions of different interpretations. In our application of this thought, we see it as a place of completeness and comfort, with "round edges and soft cushions"- a place within which your physical being can relax and permit greater thought and spiritual happiness. Each day we face constant opportunity for goodness. Too often we choose less and by this choice create our hardships.

***

Dogs, quite often, can teach us a lesson. They are so loyal and giving, constantly pouring out love to the master. No matter what the master does, or what mood he or she is in, the dog constantly pours more loving energy into them. In recent years we have all read the studies showing that people with pets live longer and fuller lives. Our lesson should be to learn to give back the same level of free love that we gain from our creature friends and those we know. There are no prerequisites or acceptable times or social norms in such a relationship-only the allowance of love.

***

Sit for a moment and permit yourself the opportunity to remember all of the best moments of your life. Review them in slow motion and recall all the people, the environment and the occasion. Next, ask yourself if all of those feelings are the same. Fulfillment is what gives us the ability to differentiate between an event and a great event, between fair and great. One way to reach the illusive 'unreachable' is to gain more understanding from all the greatness we have experienced. Spirit is the governing factor in a life of peace. 'Losers' are those without spirit. With so much energy which spirit activates, one must channel their resources so that all of their acts will end up complete and wholesome. We lose the essence of ourselves when not focusing on completion. The so-called failures or losses are established through lack of follow-through and perserverance.

***

Walt Disney was a wonderful example of a 'loser' with perseverance. As a loser he visited over a thousand banks asking them to fund his visionary, futuristic park. He was turned down more times than anyone on record. His perseverance finally led him to a kindred mind who saw the possibilities through his own healthy, active instinct. We know the rest of the story. Not only did Disney succeed in all the material ways, his vision has spread more joy throughout the world than any other person in world history.

***

Utilize your spirit. Allow it to be your shield from negativity and your strong companion in confused times. Give yourself more than you asked for so that you never can use the excuse of too little energy. All that you are is what you are willing to do. Active participating individuals are the movers and molders of the future. Being able to see clearly is not a gift; it is developed through relentless pursuit and success as well as the educator called 'failure'.

***

With my work, words are the vehicle I utilize in sparking change in people. Yet, often, the enormity of the need for that person to change cannot be stated through language. However, I have found that it can be expressed wordlessly when you permit the language of love to come from the heart through an embrace, a kiss or a hug. Maybe, in the future, when two people communicate, we can do from one heart to another, permitting our

"All that you are
is what you are
willing to do."

ultimate expression to flourish.

***

Recently, I saw a little boy speaking to his mother who had been partially paralyzed with a disease. He was showing her a drawing of himself and his mom. In it she was vigorously running and he was holding her hand. He said: "Mom, you have never been able to run with me, but I wanted to show you how our dreams can come true."

There are no paralyzed or stricken or diseased people that are not capable of transcending those difficult depths of experience. Each of us have to view ourselves as an endlessly changeable creation of a larger endlessly changeable system. If you are capable of allowing this thought to become reality, all order will come back into your life.

***

Accomplishment is no more than living that which you asked for. Are you not able to complete what you desire? Remember all the things you have already accomplished today. Look at the ways you achieved this, and become brave enough to use the same formula in your larger desires.

"Accomplishment
is no more than
living that which
you asked for."

Think, act, allow, become and BE exactly what you desire. Everything will surface when you permit your essence its freedom. Heartwarming, sensitive thoughts will permeate your life when your accomplishments become who you are, and your failures are only your teachers.

**Utilize God's wisdom as you
do your own positive thoughts.**

Chapter Three
PRACTICAL WAYS TO APPLY CONSCIOUSNESS

We are people who prepare our lives without using the wisdom of practicality. We have all been so pushed in the pursuit of knowledge that often we do not know how to formulate our daily activities. Practicality itself has a 'stick-in-the-mud' stigma and certainly does not lure us as 'vision' does.

From your adolescent years you probably remember hearing the words: "That is not practical!" Ben Franklin also heard those words when he was establishing his understanding of electricity, and the Wright Brothers heard them echo as they flew above the dunes in the Carolinas. You too can transcend the 'doomsayers' by creating practicality through completed vision.

***

You may think that mathematics is an odd bedfellow for a book on spirituality, yet here is a formula for utilizing your own capabilities to their maximum:

$$V(ision) + P(racticality) = S(uccess)$$

There are many other formulas in the ever-constant pursuit of life. This is just the most

This will help to eradicate the fairytale atmosphere that usually surrounds spirituality. Most of us have dreamer mentalities, preferring to hope for the lottery rather than to actively pursue successful human experience.

You may never truly be able to employ spirit in your life in all of its abstract and mystical ways, but, by acknowledging and then using the practical step-by-step methods toward realizing your vision, your rewards will surely come.

***

Once, when I was visiting a beautiful, peaceful, religious community in Switzerland, I asked the founder how they achieved such an environment. She looked at me and said: "It was achieved the first time I saw it in my heart. Then it was just the practical things, like building and landscaping that needed to be completed."

Recently, a similar answer came from a renowned athlete. When I asked her how she had become so good at what she does, she told me that forty years ago, when she was two years old, she had pictured herself exactly like she is today and never once wandered from that place of practicality that brought her to her desired goal. Your choice is very clear. It is one of squandered time or one of fulfillment. There are many ways

"Taking your life
to a place of spirit
is no more than
accomplishing
the things it takes
to nourish youself."

that you can reach your place of contentment but you will never achieve this without a clearly defined and empassioned life.

***

Our first step in establishing order in our lives is to truly see the humor in all that we do. This will allow us to dismiss the failing aspects and accept the more relevant ones.

Each day we should search for a theme or major reason for our lives, and let that be our guiding force in all that we do. At the end of the day, before retiring, we should acknowledge our accomplishments and review our successes. As each day passes we will gain more initiative through an actual accumulation of practicality.

Taking your life to a place of spirit is no more than accomplishing the things it takes to nourish yourself. View yourself as a child of God, and you will give yourself everything there is. So often we fear the large thoughts. This is due to our own inability to see ourselves as worthy people. Be confident that if you pursue the practical ways to your highest ambition your achievement will be assured.

***

Think of Graham Bell who believed that you could speak into a machine and somebody

"Too often our whole
 social structure is
 based upon repetitive
 patterns rather than
 the innovations
 of spirit."

miles away could exchange conversation with you.. Everyone up to that point had to rely on the written word, messenger services or the beating of a drum. Bell's conscious vision elevated the human experience, allowing us now to move on to the next level of communication. Too often our whole social structure is based upon repetitive patterns rather than the innovations of spirit. How many times have you said " I'm doing it this way because it's always been done this way"? Habitual patterns can be resting places for the weak.

***

For a period of time I had an office in New York City where I commuted to monthly from the Life-Change Center. A physician, who had been practicing natural medicine for fifty six years, was my partner at that time. Watching him deal with people brought me first-hand knowledge of letting go of all that you know to permit what is real and true. This is how each of us should conduct our lives. Often I questioned why he would suggest something diversely different from one case to another and he would smile and say " That is what the need of that person required."

"Enormity of mind
and the ability to go
beyond it are the
thresholds to God."

When my daughter was very young, she asked me why the seasons had to keep repeating themselves? In her own sweet and open mind, she asked, "If they've already done what they wanted to do, why do they have to come back again?"

We, as adults, should have the same freedom of thought that this little girl had and ask the same question of our own repetitive patterns. Maybe someday even the need for repetition will melt away due to the ability that all of us will have gained. This ability will be that of ever-expanding, limitless possibilities, and thinking these thoughts, your hearts will open wide, and your body become relaxed. Only at that time will we humans be living the life we deserve. Enormity of mind and the ability to go beyond it are thresholds to God.

***

Consider including the exercise of service in your life at least once a month. Service can be anything from an act of kindness to an heroic effort. Spend an hour in every thirty-day period immersing yourself in giving your best to someone. This assists the receiver in their elevation of consciousness, and validates your own concept of self-worth.

"Heal yourself fully
by giving to yourself
totally."

I have one friend who has volunteered at a nursing home for the last several years. This has given him the ability to feel more at peace with his own aging process, as well as given the people he has helped a better understanding of how aging does not have to mean weakening and isolation.

A whole and complete act is that of a perfect circle. All that is given out comes completely back. If you look at the larger problems in humanity, they are all due to a lack of giving. If you question this statement, for the next ten minutes ask yourself where all war, hatred and "-isms" come from. Take it to the next step and ask yourself how all of your problems have been created. In business terms, 'win/win' situations are the most desired. If we do not learn how to give, we cannot grow, any more than a flower, without sun, water and nourishing soil.

Too many of us are living to accomplish someone else's goals. If all of us were vigorously working to achieve our own with a full understanding that service is a leg on the footstool of achievement, we would all equally support one another. Heal yourself fully by giving to yourself totally. Realize your visions to gain further vision. Serve yourself completely so that you can serve all fully.

These are the wisdoms of practicality. In no way are they abstract and unreachable. They are the stepping stones to the altar of God. That place is not a place that makes us greater than others -- merely a place that makes us whole. Reach deep down into who you are and discover your own capacity to love.

***

Spirituality is not elusive. It is everything that you are doing right now to everything that you will do for the rest of your life. Do not hesitate to accept yourself as a spiritual person. Acceptance is the first act. Utilization is the second, and Practical Steps are the third.

Move on and do not question your success.

Chapter Four
FINDING THE ESSENCE OF ALL LIFE

The search for the essence of life is often confused with who we think we are. Many of our young memories from family time were discussions about our future career and the development of our own family. This has led us to focus our lives upon two different principles: economics and family responsibility. Are there not thousands of other aspects to your profoundly intricate existence? And even with that said, is that which we do the essence of who we are?

For a minute allow yourself the ability to freely arrest all preconceived notions and then turn your feelings on and search within yourself for your greatest sense of peace. This is your essence. How that relates to our physical activity makes us who we are. Sadly, most of us 'perform life' rather than live from this magnificent warmth. If you recall the greatest experience of your life, I assure you that your essence and your actions were truly harmonious then; your feelings, the result of near perfection.

If we can release our intellectual anchors, then each of us can deal with one another on an

"We are all so unified
that positive and
truthful expression
affects every drop of life."

"essence-to-essence" basis. For example, when speaking to a polite, sophisticated, mature woman, you would naturally avoid abrupt, strong language. Automatically, you know enough to change your expression and deal with her in a more suitable way. This confirms your inate ability to respond to another individual's essence.

Essence is the essential characteristic of that which makes anything what it is. Everything has an essence. And, individual essences can gather together to create a group essence that may be geographic, cultural, ethnic, or even the momentary unity of individuals caught up in an emotional experience. For example, once at a Duke Ellington concert, the entire theater and all the audience practically floated in the sky when the master and his orchestra hit the core river of their ability. It was only when the arrangement halted and Ellington, in his powerful, soft voice said: "I love you madly!" that all of us came back to our physical place. His music had just elevated us through an ecstatic group essence experience.

We are all so unified that positive and truthful expression affects every drop of life. And as we all too well understand, actions without positive essence clog the natural flow of life.

***

"Essence is that which is the pure and fulfilling perfect rhythm for every life."

For a time in my life, I conducted human-potential seminars. My objective was to demonstrate the possibilities for growth that each of us has. At the beginning of this seminar I would ask each person to express what they would do if they could do anything they desired. Inevitably, one or more would say they would go and take all of the money from a bank. As the seminar came to a close many hours later, I would ask the question again and never did one person suggest they would want to take something they had not practically worked for. This is how many of us address life...in a loose, abstract way that permits us fallacies of thought such as the easy taking of something we have not worked for.

Our essence then is our greatest friend, always permitting us the opportunity to be guided in the right direction. God's own voice echoes in this special place. When you clear your thoughts and live from your essence, all that is wise and good will come to you. This everlasting teacher will bring you to holy knowledge that dwells only in the place of truth.

Do not confuse essence with desire. Desire is that which we manufacture through a compilation of experience. Essence is that which is the pure and fulfilling perfect rhythm for every life.

***

So often we see people find themselves through the process of healing physical disease. Some years, ago a young lady with only one leg came to Florida from Europe. Although crippled, she was beautiful and kind. Our hearts filled with sympathy when she told her story of being a very successful model until she was hit by a speeding police motorcycle which severed her leg instantly, As her story went on and she spoke of coming out of the coma which her doctor had said would kill her, her eyes lit up and she smiled radiantly. Her words came from her essence when she said: "Now I know what significance my life has. I will spend the rest of my life giving to those in need." Within seconds after her miraculous rebirth, she went from a successful model to a successful human being who now shares her spirit with people worldwide. We can change, and we will improve if we only embrace who we really are.

Recently, an actor who had enjoyed an active career came to an abrupt change of consciousness when he pulled himself from the depths of disaster into a wheelchair that became a throne of wisdom. Overnight he became the voice of faith and hope and the perfect example of human potential.

"Do not allow life to be
a series of confused acts.
Create your life as a theater
of competent action."

Within you is the same voice that has been graciously bestowed upon us by a benevolent God. Not one minute goes by in your life when you are not capable of being totally in your essence. All of those problems that you may presently perceive as unsolvable can be your motivation to transformation.

So often we become lost intentionally so that we do not have to deal with the vividly clear essence. Our own capacity is squashed by the fear of who we are.

Do you remember those times when you were willing to do exactly what your heart desired? These memories are easy to access since they are the times when, guided by your essence, you lived life well. Magic is not manufactured. It is alive and present in those that live their essence.

Within each step on your way to an essence-filled life you may be assured that your guidance is enormous and without hesitation. Fully understand all that you have done and then you will better understand where you need to go. Do not allow life to be a series of confused acts. Create your life as a theatre of competent action.

***

Many years ago, someone told me a story about the great composer, Rachmaninoff. Often

"Our true mastery of life is not that of what we can do, but that of what we may allow."

after leaving the keyboard he would say to an associate or friend, "Wasn't it interesting what was done tonight?" By viewing his performance more as the spectator rather than the master, he dwelled in the place that all of us need to be. When we are there, we give to ourselves without pretense or control. We then can accept ourselves as part of an endless chain of connecting lives. Our true mastery of life is not that of what we can do, but that of what we may allow.

***

In each of our times we can gather enough momentum to bestow change on a stagnant world. Our driven heart can spill truth into the present minds and the future generations. The great writers, musicians and leaders are not the only ones given this opportunity. It is equally your opportunity to contribute to all there is. This contribution is not one that you should desire, but one you should permit, because without fail every one of us has this within us.

***

Give yourself five minutes at the end of each day where you are as peaceful as possible, without words and without memory or thought.

within those magic moments who you are can surface so that you can romance your true self and look forward to a life-long love affair with the heart rather than the head.

***

On our grounds here at the Institute, we once had a peacock fly in and spend two years with us. Shortly after he arrived, I brought in a peahen as his partner. Together they "talked" and played and ate and shared their days with us. So many of our guests from all over the globe spent hours of pleasure watching the natural elegance of their lives. I often thought that all of us could be like the peacocks, but most of us doubt our own ability to be so magnificent. Choosing the possibility of being magnificent makes us grow beyond our self-imposed limits and accept our potential. Aligning our purposes with our essence makes it possible to reach a place of total fulfillment.

***

Kindness is an example of what all of our actions should be, and willingness is what all thought should be. There are many other ingredients in the pursuit of living but each of these ingredients are dependent upon one another, so together they will bring you a life of happiness. Within the history of all things is the knowledge that can allow us to harvest the fruitful soul of life. The conclusion of your life is a spiritual event which is made of your history,-- true history-- not perceived, not invented. It may be that your greatest contribution is that you leave this world with a smile on your face and a pocketful of goodness.

***

The essence of life is the essence of YOU. So, BE it, and enjoy it.

Chapter Five
THE HEART OF ALL THOUGHT

Have we not missed one of the most important aspects of our life: the reality that all thought existed before it entered into our physical realm? The heart of all thought comes from a place outside ourselves. Once encapsulated in our minds, we can then translate thoughts into the actions of our lives.

***

Recently, a friend described a trip they had taken to a large health food store, recreating the two hours that she spent flowing up and down the rivers of aisles. "I don't know what made me pick certain foods," she said, "but they just seemed so appealing." We can relate this to the way we permit thought to enter into our realm of acceptance. In the invisible float the words of God, and also the most vile and disgusting of all ideas. Like a great market of abundant choices, this illustrious element of the human experience can bring us our greatest joy when our selection is wise and considered. It is for us to sensitize ourselves to that which we will accept as part of our own person and choose only what is wholesome and most nourishing for our lives.

"Your conscious choices
can be the dialogue
with your soul that will
permit you the grace
of a smooth life."

For most of my life, I felt I had little or no control over what came into my mind. Blaming it on my past haunting memories, I would permit negativity to permeate my very existence. Then several years ago, a joyful acquaintance who was 103 years old, said to me, that he loved being alive because he had more time to think about all the wondrous things. His words intrigued me until I finally understood that he had consciously chosen to accept only the powerfully important thoughts of harmony and happiness. And with this he had dismissed the angry detractors of spirit.

Some may suggest that we have to allow the worst thoughts into our lives to acknowledge the importance of the positive ones. Others propose a more utopian idea that says we should contain and utilize only the finest thoughts. Just as many people seem to need struggle and hardship to recognize the importance of effort, while others breeze through life, always smiling and content, always acknowledging how privileged they have become. This all depends upon the way you choose to teach yourself how to live a better life and your life will reflect your choices! That is the governing factor in all we have discussed in this writing -- your conscious choices can be the dialogue with your soul that will permit you the grace of a

*The careless misuse
of thought can take us
into the dark waters
of negativity and sadness."*

smooth life. Thought can be like a sail on a windy day, and the rudder that guides us steadily in the direction we desire. But the careless misuse of thought can take us into the dark waters of negativity and sadness.

***

Let's take a moment to go through an exercise so we can see how easy it is to dismiss unwanted thoughts. Begin by sitting comfortably in an environment that is restful. Close your eyes and slowly take ten very deep breaths, letting them in and out slowly. Place in your mind the most unpleasant thing you can think of. Then superimpose a picture of the time that you totally and absolutely fell in love. Try to let both thoughts become as strong as they can. Sit for as long as it takes and you will feel the negative melt away. Love will always win. This inevitable result is due to primary laws that govern all life. Negativity is halting to progress. The very thing that prevents you from success cunningly hides itself in the fear to which it gives birth. Whereas pure goodness from positive thought is the activator of the universe...the heart of all creation. Without the unseen world of positive consciousness we would not have life.

***

Not long ago a lovely woman addressed a group of people I was sitting with. Her subject was the experience she had with a bird house when she was a child. She had constructed the birdhouse and waited, watching it through her window for one whole year before a mother bird chose the little house as her home. That special day, when the tiny bird flew in with straw in her mouth, was the beginning of her understanding the 'heart of all thought'. Day after day she watched the little bird, slowly and carefully weaving together a secure and comfortable nest for her soon-to-be babies. And when the chicks arrived, making themselves known with wondrous chirping, the mother continued to openly give 100% of herself. The child watched them grow until they finally flew away with the mother bird, into the wider world of their natural life.

As a child, this lady had witnessed 'the heart of all thought' in the simple fact that the mother bird had only permitted the vision of her babies' needs to govern her every action. Without doubt or hesitation from this unswerving focus, she had been capable of providing all that was necessary for life to unfold perfectly, as it was designed to do.

***

Perhaps you will ask how we can moderate thought that has become part of our physical person. This calls for more creativity and understanding. As an example: All of us have certain ideas about how something should be done. This has been established through habitual procedures over a period of time. When we have experienced this continual repetitive process enough we accept it as 'our way.' Does it always mean that it is the only way, or the best way? It could possibly be incorrect or even absurd. Even if by some chance we actually are thinking well, so that many of the things that we repeatedly do are, for now, the 'best', there is no doubt that many of the things we think and do are quite far off from optimum. We have just not become aware of the gap. This is where thought that has become synthesized into habit becomes challenging. Here's an example:

One of our guests at the Life-Change Center told a story about a job he had as a young man. At seventeen he became a housepainter's apprentice. Each morning, he was handed a bucket and a brush and was sent to paint one side of a house. He vigorously proceeded to paint with as much energy as he had in himself. When

"Become an active member of the human race by using all of your faculties."

lunchtime came he would walk around to the other side of the house, and see that his boss had painted ten times more than he had. This went on for weeks without his boss once suggesting that there was a problem. Finally, he gathered enough courage to ask his boss to show him how he could paint so fast. " First," his boss said, "show me how *you* paint." And then after watching him for a minute, he took the brush and started to make wide, gentle, vertical strokes. But when the brush was returned to him, the young man could not get the same results though he tried time after time. Then his boss said, "Your arm will not hurt as much if you just let it move freely." And that was the key! Shortly after this, they often met at lunch having evenly accomplished their painting tasks.

This is how many of us work within the confines of thought. If only we could elevate our awareness to the level that would allow us the easy, successful way of proceeding. Dreaming about it will not really get you anywhere. You must use all your power to challenge your most ingrained habits, and when finding that they are not your highest possible choice, permitting yourself to let them go. You must re-establish, through new thought, the best way of conducting your life. This endless triad of challenge, release and replace should continue throughout life. As we grow and age, our thoughts can continue to change with honor.

**

Today I was listening to a delightful interview with a musical actor who had portrayed Gershwin's first Porgy. He was now in his nineties, and a genuine light of intelligence and sophistication. The interviewer asked how Gershwin had presented the opportunity to him and he described how the composer had come to his apartment in Washington, and played the music for him. He recalled how, while listening, his eyes had lit up and his spirit flowed with the music. "As an African-American," the performer said, "I had expected it to lack the feeling of persuasion of my people, yet I found it to be a respectful and genuine portrayal of my culture. And at that moment I knew I had to be part of this work." As the interview went on, he was asked if the most important thing he had ever done was to play this role and if this was how he wanted to be remembered? He answered, "I truly want to be remembered as a man who had a full and successful life doing what I loved to do." His thoughts were so well defined that we listeners understood deeply that life can be personally significant when we make the right choices.

***

Ironically, the same mind that can assist you to greatness will question your motivation for doing so. Arrest and erradicate the spoilers of imagination so that your ability to envision will not be impaired.

If we could only fill our heads with kindness and compassion every minute of our lives, we would all have a remarkable existence. Compassion relates to understanding all. Become an active member of the human race by using all of your human faculties. This is not something uniquely bestowed upon a privileged few. It is an ocean available to all swimmers.

Reaching this place of free thought is quite possible when you are willing to take yourself less seriously. The very significance you have created around yourself is the armor that prevents the penetration of God's words from the invisible. This armor acts as a magnet for negative thought and further strengthens the pretentious person that you have so intellectually pieced together. It may be difficult for you to get from the place where you are now to a place of open willingness. Without this occurrence, it will only be an average life with acceptable standards. Perhaps one in which your

"Until you get rid of anger,
fear, hostility and hatred,
you are still diseased."

epitaph would read "Here lies a good person who did his best." Would it not be better for it to read: "This person did everything possible to stretch the limits of his best." For with the gift of life we are obligated to vigorously pursue our higher purpose, and falling short of this weakens our self-image. With this weakening we are permitting the invasion of human sickness on all levels.

I have often stated when addressing gatherings, " You may have gotten rid of cancer, but until you get rid of anger, fear, hostility and hatred, you are still very diseased." This is an enormous challenge since the substance of history has been based on who wins, who gains, who controls. Our very system of values is based on material accomplishments that were gathered together through imperfect thinking. These are the things that rip the heart out of a spiritual existence.

***

The tapestry of eternal thought which is woven through the centuries is a Garden of Eden. When the real essence of who you are can be expressed clearly through spiritual thought, it will guide you to your highest possibilities in life.

***

The heart of all thought is the heart
that each of us deserves--
one of capacity beyond belief and
ability beyond imagination.

Chapter Six
MAKING LIFE WORK

Making life work is far easier than most of us know. There are three principles that govern our lives: physical, emotional and mental/spiritual.

First, consider the **physical** principle which is quite easy to describe since it is solidly visible and largely understood. Underneath the heading of the physical, there are three basic subcategories:

1) Cell structure - which is not only the billions of tiny round objects floating through you, but also the outer surface of your skin and everything you see and know inside.

2) The fuel, or food of these cells and tissues. Under this subhead there are 6 basic foods: oxygen, water, food we eat and drink, sunlight, exercise (aerobic and resistant), and rest.

3) The third principle of life (generally placed incorrectly under the emotions) includes negative influences such as: Fear, Anger, and Hatred. All of these affect bodily function in that their absence conditions health or their presence permits the harboring of disease. When you synthesize only the positive aspects of the physical in your life and put forth your utmost committment to all of these basic necessities, your body will be

"Those people who learn to change gracefully are the most successful and emotionally balanced."

your friend.

***

The second principle of life is the **emotional.** Your whole person reacts to all that you experience based on your understanding of self and others. From our parents, our teachers, our religious leaders, we have heard that there is some wonderous plateau we can reach where our life comes into total balance. This is truly a lovely thought, but not the truth of life. Parents who are consciously in tune would explain to you that all there is in life is change, and that those people who learn to change gracefully are the most successful and emotionally balanced.

***

The logic in not trying to prevent change came to me many years ago when I went on a sabbatical in southern Oregon. In the summer when it was over 100° F, the local people taught me to jump in the river and totally relax my body so that I could float with and through nature. After many attempts, my body, rigid with fear, finally returned to its normal state. Floating then gave me a magical connection to God's earth, heightened my senses and brought me to a true sense of the power of the spirit. On the third river float, feeling more calm and conscious than ever in my life, I turned for one second against the river

> *"Abstaining*
> *from your spirit*
> *is your greatest loss."*

and instantly found myself desperately struggling to avoid drowning. When I finally managed to drag myself to the shore, I had learned a new lesson. Rivers are like life. Most of us are not wise enough to relax and go with it. To fight against the river is to be overwhelmed by its power. When we fight against the natural flow of life, this is when we become spiritually and emotionally sick. Getting in tune with your emotions is not about you controlling what happens, but more about you giving in to God.

***

Third - are the **mental and spiritual** elements that make life work. They are your understanding of God and how you relate to the Higher in your life. This combination is the foundation of what this book is attempting to bring you. The marriage of spirituality into your every thought will eliminate your failures and gently mold a life of peaceful strength. Abstaining from your spirit is your greatest loss. And yet many people work very hard to ignore or disavow this divine energy that is within each of our souls. Spirit is the place where your credibility will be challenged. Clear and defined questions come to mind when accepting your spiritual aspect. Most relevant is the question: "Are you willing to give your life to God?"

"The laws of existence
always work
when we surrender
to spirit."

We are not suggesting that you have to become a crusader. The inner surrender to the Higher is enough. This quiet and profound act will allow you the power to go beyond your basic physical capabilities.

***

Not so long ago, I visited with a friend who confided that for many years he had dreamed of doing fine woodwork but never felt he had enough artistic ability. Finally, he realized that when he had blockages in other areas of his life he would call on God for help. Whenever this was done with true earnestness, he would achieve his goal. Off he went carving and cutting and proceeding with faith. Well into the story I stopped him and asked if he had achieved his goal. He laughed and said, "You're sitting in it right now" What a comfortable, artistic chair!

***

The laws of existence always work when we surrender to spirit, let go of our blockages, smooth our emotions and fuel our body with all the necessary nutriments and actions. Struggle comes when these primary aspects are ignored or only partially dealt with. You may feel that you can go on without acknowledging these elements, yet it has been proven countless times that it is not possible.

The laws of existence, formulated at the beginning of life, like the flow of the river, direct us unerringly to our greatest fulfillment.

Continue always to expand your understanding of the great natural laws of life, and always be in pursuit of your dreams.

Make your life work!

Chapter Seven
WHO WILL ANSWER YOUR DREAMS?

Both our night dreams and our daydreams are secret friends. Even our nightmares contain maps for opportunity. Sadly, we do not have a format in education or spiritual teaching which addresses dreams well, although scientists have shown us over the years that if we do not permit people to use fantasy, their mental capacity and physical health will suffer. In actuality, the only propeller to our future are our dreams themselves.

***

When Hippocrates Health Institute was located in Boston, we had a Harvard professor who taught in our program. He was an expert in interpreting dreams. Our guests often clamored around him in hopes of discovering more about themselves. Watching his interaction with them, I saw that he always made it a pleasing experience, and by the time he had finished weaving together both the inner and the outer dreams, the person he was addressing had visibly grown in self-esteem.

But, do we need personal interpreters to discover what it is we would really like to do? Can we not start to acknowledge for ourselves

"Your experience and
your potential are
the ingredients
that create a dream."

these vivid keys to our abilities?

***

Children act on their dreams so freely each and every day. Take the time to sit quietly and observe youngsters at play. Listen to the conversations they have with their invisible friends, and most of all, comprehend how much joy they are having.

You too can transfer your highest aspirations into your greatest actions. Only conditioning of the mind can prevent you from living your dreams. Only you can determine your true desires. These desires are revealed in your dreams.

***

For a moment think about the wildest things that you have ever fantasized. Then ask yourself why these thoughts were gathered together by your mind. Do they have the same origin as your other thoughts, or are they pieced together from your deepest memories? With a dream you can say yes to both of these ideas. Your experience and your potential are the ingredients that create a dream.

One may ask how this is possible when some of the things you fantasize about are so radically different from your own life experiences.

*"You too can transform
your highest aspirations
into your greatest actions."*

We have seen time and again that people with an interesting and intricate past have enormous ability to create phenomenal dreams while people with a shallow and limited history tend to dream in a more conservative fashion. How much we dare to dream has to do with the natural rhythms of life itself and how much of it we will allow ourselves to participate in.

*****

To get a sense of how the energy of dreams can expand for the dreamer, imagine for a moment being at an african dance. First the quiet and then, suddenly, begins the pounding of drums. The dancers take their first steps and begin to move into the rhythms of their soul. Slowly you feel your own energy heighten until you are caught up in an uncontrollable desire to move. As the music continues and the dancers heat up, your energy continues to heighten with the music and the movement. So it is with our dreams. They can also gather energy, heighten and expand as we move with them in response to the natural rhythms of our soul.

God encourages us to aspire to greatness and fully supports our mission to accomplish our goals. Your life will be enriched by permitting the constantly available dreams to be acknowledged and used, to grow and expand, rather than be squashed and eliminated.

I hear people claim that none of their dreams ever come true. When I ask them why they feel this way, the word failure always permeates the conversation. The concept that we call failure and the fear of it, is a dam that prevents the naturally occurring flow of life. Too many of us create our own restrictions through fearful and negative thinking. Those self-constructed inhibitors become self-inflictors. They jumble our time and confuse our actions. If you find yourself in the middle of doing something that you have no desire to do yet you continue on with it, realize that you are creating an even higher dam that prevents the usage of your dreams.

***

When Thomas Edison was in the middle of his inventive work, a young admirer complimented him on his brilliance: "Look at all the wonderful things you have invented." During a rare moment of tenderness Edison explained to the young lad that for every invention that worked, there had been numerous failures before the success. What is the difference between Thomas Edison and you?

***

"When we do not utilize
our greatness,
we lose our capabilities."

Not too long ago, I spoke to a young lady who had been crippled by an accident and now was living in a wheelchair. When I spoke to her, I painted a verbal picture of the day that she would be married and how wonderful it would be as she danced at her own wedding surrounded by family and friends. She smiled radiantly and asked if she could really do that someday. I said, "Of course, you can! But you have to learn how to reach out and capture all that you desire."

One of our great gifts is the ability we have to receive all in a positive way. Too often we forget this and do not stand vigilance to protect this enormous asset. When we do not utilize our greatness, we lose our capabilities.

***

As humans we need our dreams. It is our innate instinct to fantasize -- to combine our past and our future is healing to the mind which brings us greater consciousness. Have you noticed that when you've had too little sleep you feel an annoying absence of energy in your head? This is due to the lack of feeding that your consciousness lost through the absence of dreams.

Dancing with dreams will bring back the kind of delightful feelings that you may have had on a summer's day as a child. It will also elevate you to a place of freedom and happiness that is really easy to reach...without struggle, without effort. We have all been taught so very well to ignore the finest aspects of who we are. Our dreams, positive thought, esssence, etc., are all fundamental to a life that is worth living.

***

A lady of great musical genius confided that she was always slightly depressed whenever she was not engaged in her art. When I asked her why she didn't continue on a daily basis to play and perform, she said it was because she had always been taught that she needed to rest. This example clearly shows us that at times what looks logical is not the best. What is rewarding and fulfilling always is. Having the knowledge that you may accept a life with deep and wholesome dimensions will permit you to reach endless potential. Exhaustion will never occur when you become exhilarated through fulfilling actions.

***

Increasing your future is as primary to life as drinking water is to your physical body. God is within that future, and it is for you to both reach for and accomplish all your positive deeds. Incorrectly manipulating your future can cut you off from further possibility. Somewhere deep

> "Infinite
> is too small a word
> for the possibilities
> we each can harness."

down inside you know that everything is fine, because surrounding you is all the energy that you need.

***

In the days of early television there was a character named Maynard G. Krebs. He was a bohemian who always displayed profound thoughts lightly. In one episode he pondered the grains of salt in a shaker and wondered if maybe all of the planets and even the entire universe might actually be inside one of those grains.

Just like Maynard, most of our comfort levels need a beginning and an end. This falsely enables us to think that we can finally reach a utopian plateau and then our life will be perfect. Would it not be more honest to understand that there are no starts and finishes? There is only the all available, all giving, all knowing and all capable. It does not have to be in a square or a circle, or in the clouds or deep in the earth. Infinite is too small a word for the possibilities we each can harness.

Your choice is not hard. It is clearly available when you permit yourself to gain from your deepest instinct. This capacity is limitless because as you grow and accept more of your ability, the capacity will expand.

Imagine yourself as a clean, new blackboard. And now make a defined decision that nothing will ever be written on the board except positive words that come from harmonious thoughts. Then clearly decide that each of those words will join together into sentences that will lead you in the direction of a great future. Now recognize where the blackboard and the words have come from. one external. one internal. Dreams are made from these very things

***

Abstract philosophies have thrown us off track when it comes to the practical use of vital elements. As interesting as some things may be, nothing matches the interest you will gain when you make your dreams come true. How else do you expect yourself to be happy? Not your closest friend, your husband, wife, or child can accomplish your happiness. This must come from honest and rich preparation that will turn your life back over to you. Once you are responsible, you will freely commit yourself to resting in the arms of God. Those people who do so are like cups that have a continual flow coming from them. You not only will be filled and nourished with the warm and perfect feeling that you deserve, you will also help to fill the often empty cups of those you touch.

Look through history and think about some of our finest contributors to the human experience. These are ever-flowing energy givers. Decades or hundreds or thousands of years after their passing, their energies still radiate.

Conscious kind acts towards yourself will enrich the whole human race. When you permit yourself to plug in to God, your symphony will begin. Do not allow yourself to play solo, since it will inevitably exhaust you.

Who will answer your dreams?
You will, in co-creation with God.

Chapter Eight

CREATING OPPORTUNITY/ ALLOWING SUCCESS

Opportunity is of such interest to all of us that we often miss the message it brings. Incorrectly, we feel that it comes to us by chance and that there is no connection between our needs and its creation. We must understand that opportunity is attracted to us and carved by us and that success is not possible without opportunity first. Our oportunities come from the place where our desires live, and are partners to our needs.

It is for us to recognize opportunity when it appears and determine what the message is. Too often we neglect to acknowledge that first step in achieving success. We somehow believe that we can reach our goals without a step-by-step plan toward our desired success. Opportunity presents itself as a stairway to creation.

I often see that people who are ill, do not understand their disease to be an opportunity. It certainly does not look like something that would lead us to success, and instead has all the earmarks of pain and failure. Disease is the greatest example of the way our personal efforts can bring us to a new level of fulfillment.

Week after week, year after year, we have guests who come in admiration of our teaching. Their hope is that we will make them well. We know that they are the only ones who have the possibility of doing that themselves. When they acknowledge this and work to accomplish their own healing, they then become *our* teachers.

This incredible linking of personal opportunities that bring success is working in every area of your life. Spend time searching for your direction through your need. Do not allow your needs to be your enemies. They are only there to bring you happiness.

***

When I was teaching in a third world country, I was appalled to find out that some of the children maimed themselves so that they could be beggars. With my value system, this was unthinkable, and in a deep way, disturbing. One very hot afternoon, I was approached by a ten-year old boy on crutches who was missing his right leg. Through a translator I asked him how he lost his leg. And he told me, smiling, that he had ' lost it to make money.' This boy's perception of opportunity and success had inflicted permanent damage on him. His need for money had been stronger than his need for mobility.

"Of all things that are destructive,
our lack of wisdom on how we should proceed is paramount."

Choices against need come up in your life every day. The wrong choice can change your life for the worst. The right choices can guide you to greatness.

***

A bird in the north, responding to a seasonal signal, spreads its wings and flies south. The raindrops in a torrential downpour gather on the earth and rapidly flow toward sealevel. They are both following natural laws.

You will also go naturally in a direction that is right for you when you permit opportunities into your life. Confusion prevails when we do not see our abilities. Fear reigns when we stop in the center of negative thought. And of all things that are destructive, our lack of wisdom on how we should proceed is paramount.

So often we see others succeed and wonder why we do not have their luck. This word, luck, must have been thought up by the world's greatest pessimist. This thought is not from a holy place that enriches your life. It carries the seeds of loss and defeat. All is possible, and there is no luck.

Gather yourself together and take the steps necessary to come to the place you so desire. When you arrive there, thank God for the opportunity that brought you success, for as we reach our goals we must humbly acknowledge the accomplishment so that more opportunities will surface.

***

For many years, I wondered how we could enlarge the dining area at the institute for our guests. Day after day and year after year my mind was taxed by this problem and the answer never came. There was always the recurrent thought that there seemed to be limited space, lack of funds or absence of workmen. After seven years, a gentleman who knew my concern walked me over to a big window at the end of the dining area. In one minute he explained to me that a door could be created here leading out into a large screened patio enclosure. He introduced me to the opportunity that I could not see in front of my own eyes for years.

***

How often have you found yourself caught in the web of lethargy that permeates failure? This is a place where decay begins and spreads to all parts of our life. Break out of the grip of inaction. There are so many great events waiting to happen. Give yourself a chance to experience them. Creating opportunity is a simple matter of acknowledging that all that you do should have the quality within it that success requires. I have a formula for this that will make you laugh. It is called 'getting GAS':

G+A=S

(Goals plus Actions equal Success.)

Think of this kind of gas as the high test fuel for your life.

***

My son has a gift in preparing food. As a child he constantly asked if he could prepare meals. At that time we were reluctant to have him help and discouraged him from doing so. When we finally gave our permission, weren't we surprised when we tasted his delicious vegetable dishes! This is an example of how others may try to prevent your opportunity.

Your own persistence in pursuing success should conjure up enough courage in you to be unwavering in your mission. If you found yourself desperately swimming in the middle of the ocean, and you saw a life preserver floating ninety feet away, would you hesitate in your efforts to reach it? You have life preservers spread out on your journey through life. Discover the comfort they will bring you when you rest in them, but never forget that you may act at the same time that you are feeling secure.

"Here is where you have
gained knowledge,
and there is where you
must go."

It is like note after note that creates music -- a continuous piece that plays throughout life *Here* is where you have gained knowledge and *there* is where you must go. Give yourself everything you need to understand every thing there is. And while accomplishing this feat do not wallow in the mere fact that you have reached a bit of understanding. Remember that this is only one step in the pursuit.

We are taught mathematical formulas in school such as 8+8=16. When we accomplish the understanding that 16 is the answer, we are then drawn on to master the next set of questions and answers for more understanding. In other areas of our lives we do not seem to comprehend as readily the absolute demand placed on us to continue. We often move our whole life from one place to another, expecting that action alone to accomplish all the answers. But if we neglect to continue actively seeking ever more understanding, we will be denying our capacity for growth.

***

Throughout history there have been oppressed and downtrodden people. All of the visible signs would show little hope for them. Then we see one unique individual rise above the illusion of hopelessness and seize the opportunities

"Recall all of your
former successes
and you will find the keys
to the door of
future successes."

that exist.

As we aspire to reach great places, we create jewels...the rich gifts that are brought to us through our own efforts. Dreamers who have the grace to proceed with actions will fill their lives completely. Vision and committment lead them to the treasurehouse of opportunities. Everything in life is available as needed. Attract those things that are tools of knowledge and reject those that are motivators of fear. There is no problem. There are no limits. You *can* do everything necessary.

***

One day I asked a friend of mine who was a counsellor if she would share the secret of her great success in helping people to change their lives. She sat back smiling and gave me this: "When I'm with people for one hour, I say nothing but an occasional 'a ha', for fifty minutes. During this time I write down all the positive things they have said about themselves. In the last ten minutes this is what we discuss and focus on." She was wise enough to see that people are their successes. Their opportunities come from this very place. Her wisdom brings us to understand the ease of finding rich opportunities.

Recall all of your former successes and you will find the keys to the door of future successes.

> *"In our sophistication*
> *we dim our ability*
> *to see the simple things."*

Too often we try to build our lives on the shaky ground of our inabilities, based on pretentious and exaggerated expectations of who we think we are. By overlaying the knowledge of what we can do (because we've already done it) and peeling away the layers of 'cannot', we will reach a place of absolutes.

In our sophistication we dim our ability to see the simple things. The clouds gathering rain can bring about success. The snowstorm that stops progress may also bring success, and even the book that you've just read, with passages that you didn't quite understand will reward you.

Do not think that opportunity will just fall into your lap with no effort, but put all of yourself into the committment that you will actively achieve success - and then *allow yourself to enjoy every minute of it!*

Chapter Nine
Finding A Way To Eternal Life

Eternity is more than we can ever imagine. There is no evidence that eternity even exists although in every single religion of the world there is discussion of eternity, and deep down all of us know that life does not end. In observing nature we see the continual change of seasons and the rotation of the earth.

Looking back through history, we can see the great accomplishments of the past. The discovery of the wheel, as an example, brought us to a new found mobility, and today wheels are on the rocket ships we send into space.

Embracing the essence of the great words, even from millenniums past, can help us to create our future. There may have been a time when these thoughts would feel uncomfortable to you since they do not give us viability in our own achievements. We would like to think of reaching a final place of accomplishment where our lives could rest. But do not limit yourself in the belief that there is any ultimate event. Give yourself the gift of continual achievement.

While I was studying science I was so surprised to find out how long it took for the light we see in the stars to reach us. This endless flow of electrical charge is what carries the spark of all life.

***

One day while I was walking on the coast of Maine, I found a bottle with a note in it that had been written in 1936. It was in French and had come from an island far south in the Carribean. This taught me one of the basic laws of eternal thought...the action of release and sending out. Can you feel your own significance without the need to harbor it? Can you let go of all the visible things that you think of as important, in the assurance that your next steps will fill you with greater harmony?

We've all been taught with a reward system in mind, convinced that achievement will result in success. Yet, your perception is what evaluates your own successes. Further, you have to pile success upon success while Eternity, as a proprosition of continuous life, smiles and beckons to you, encouraging you to always go further without reward in mind.

***

Public broadcasting TV recently aired a documentary filmed in the Himalayas. An Oxford expedition was there to find the Shangri-La that

"Give of yourself freely
and lovingly
to gain all of the insight
that is necessary
to comfort you on your
journey."

had long been acknowledged by the locals in that area of the world. Slowly, they climbed higher and higher, going through many villages that were filled with monasteries and spritual places. Finally they climbed to a place absent of man's structures, and there the guides announced that they had reached utopic Shangri-La. For the intellectuals of the expedition it was quite difficult to accept that there could be anything of significance where there was no trace of man. Slowly, the gentle, calm feeling that pervaded the environment raised the consciousness of these travelers who finally realized that there was no need for monuments here. This was a place where people came to find eternal peace. You may find this in your church, your temple, your synagogue or in your park.

All of us experience the lure of eternity every day in our own lives . It is the strong magnet that pulls us forward in spite of our own lack. Conception to birth, to living, to passing, is merely a small part of all there is. Our souls go forward, both contributor and encourager. Give yourself the joy of pursuing the passionate place that we all must seek. Give of yourself freely and lovingly to gain all of the insight that is necessary to comfort you on your journey..

For a long-distance runner who knows at the starting line that he has many miles to run, the concept of eternity may be quite daunting, yet the winner at the finish line finds eternity a welcome thought.

We can develop a friendship with the inevitable when we are willing to dismiss our physical need of acquiring. We must utilize all that is accessible to us for the one and only goal of continuance. Many of the struggles we humans experience are due to the need we have of collecting without reason.

We have so often seen our priorities skewed when it comes to a focused life. We have forgotten the keys to abundant success, happiness, fulfillment, love, contentment. These are really your primary objectives. How is it that you have gotten so far off track and assumed that all else around you is more important?

Your entire life is a mission of self-discovery and constant release, like a holding pond where waters flow in and out. God gives you the opportunities you require. Sometimes in this holding pond we grab onto a leaf, or twig that may be floating there and find ourselves going around and around in circles, without the ability to move forward. We get caught in whirlpools of habitual actions. To break out of that, get up and sing a song when it seems inappropriate, go for a long walk when you are tired, watch a funny movie when you're sad.

People tend to repeat their mistakes since they are uncomfortable with the movement forward. The unknown region brings great anxiety to those who are not free enough to live the truth.

Your entry to eternity is based on the quality of your thoughts, actions, and spirituality. When you use these tools well, your experience will be that of a clear mission. If you fail to use integrity in these areas, you will feel out of touch and confused. There is never an instant when you are truly lost. Within an inch of where you are is the answer to your future. This future is accessible to you when you choose to believe in eternity as your guide.

Knowledge is always available when you are willing to let go. Your struggle comes from your belief that you think you know something. To eliminate the struggle, understand that you must release the 'think' part and accept that you 'know'. How often have you found yourself rapidly making the right decision and then when thinking about it for a minute, you assemble a wrong idea. These are all blocks to eternal life.

"There is never an instant
when you are truly lost.
Within an inch of where
you are is the answer
to your future."

You may live this eternity right now when you are passsionate about all, free-falling, openly joyous, with the understanding that creation is here for you to enjoy. Jump like a child, give like a philanthropist, know from wisdom, and love from the heart and all will be well.

Quite simple, yet profound examples of what you should do are written in the center of your spiritual life. Your interpretation depends upon your ability to access the unknown.

Trust is hard for those who do not believe deeply. As we mentioned early on, many people wait for signs before proceeding. How sad it is that their faith is so limited that they require some assurance before they are willing to trust.

***

Once a guest asked how they would know when they had reached a place of total health. I suggested that they think about a powerful waterfall that pours from the side of a high cliff. This is the feeling you have when you are vibrant and filled with true health. I asked them to close their eyes and see this waterfall, endlessly flowing, continually moving, forever falling, without a place to collect, never filling a pool. This is how your life should proceed. This is how life is eternally proceeding, either with or without you.

"Quite simple, yet profound
examples of what you
should do
are written in the center
of your spiritual life."

Over the years it has been interesting to me to see that limited thinking creates limited success. Within our own hearts we can design a system of living that will bring us the strength to want to go further and further without hesitation. As this proceeds, we will desire a more rapid movement into inevitable eternity.

All that is worth doing is in the hands of worthy people. Worthiness is not selected by God, rather, it lies in the opportunity they have of accepting it. Mankind is at a place with more possibilities and larger capacities than we ever have had before. Everything is possible and nothing is limited. Given the circumstance the mighty believers will flourish like flowers in spring, and the fearful will wither in the burning sun. Commit yourself now to be all-loving. Centuries of madness should not anchor you into passive participation. It is for you to break the shackles and annoint yourself as an eternal person. Accepting God is not a courageous act. It is an all-absorbing and ever-giving act.

We are fundamentally ridiculous when it comes to our own concept of how we should proceed. There is no doubt that when you reach a place of knowing what this is all really about, your heart will be filled with acceptance. Every day

> *"Ease is the result
> of a wise existence."*

repeat to yourself that everything is fine and all will result in success as long as you are ready to acknowledge eternity.

***

I asked a minister who had practiced for forty-nine years what he felt his greatest accomplishment was. He said simply that it was reaching a place of "total release of Self."

Accomplishing this will enable you to gain your roadmap to eternity. Without effort you will be able to interpret all of your actions and determine how you can make them better and easier. Ease is the result of a wise existence. If you are doing anything that is a great struggle you can be sure you are not on the right track. Because of our discardable mentality, we permit ourselves to let go of anything that is difficult. This is certainly the wrong approach. We must refine our ability to perceive things with great vision. This will allow us to apply ourselves so that all will come easily.

***

Have you ever noticed how a fine artist can paint such beautiful objects on a piece of canvas? The vibrance of the painting can even capture the essence of the objects. It is so easy to the artist, and so pleasing to all of us. This is how life should go. Contribution after contribution,

*"Gain from your acceptance
of God,
and permit your joy
to affect others."*

from perceptually clear individuals who do not fail to act correctly in any instance.

***

You can reach eternal life by living it today -- never asking for more than you need --always encouraged to participate with everything that touches you. Sensibly free, gloriously giving, your abilities will become endless gifts.

Somewhere on your journey you will capture your spirit, so as to give it away a little bit at a time. Gain from your acceptance of God and permit your joy to affect others. Only through positive action can you affect the whole. There are no battles to win, and nothing to conquer when your struggle comes down to release. Stand for all that is significant but reach a place where defense is not necessary. Quiet your words and display kindness and compassion when negativity reaches your door.

**Do not judge others;
only acknowledge God,
and eternity will bring you
the happiness you deserve.**

Chapter Ten

THE PRINCIPLES OF SPIRITUAL EXISTENCE

The principles of spiritual existence are without question your great guides to a life that is worth living. Written like an alphabet, they are there for you to learn from, as a living language. As you enlarge your repretoire each aspect gains momentum and eventually your ability to have more grace becomes permanent. Hand in hand with God, you will then comfortably move through your days and years with the ease of a butterfly in a beautiful garden.

Spirituality is not a set of rules and regulations that constrict or limit us. It is really the totality of endless potential. Our co-creation of life is generated by the very essence of spirituality. Universally we are all connected and eventually we will eliminate the illusion of separation. With this knowledge you face a fearless future.

Never categorize spirituality as something that you utilize occasionally. There is no fulfillment without constant acceptance of this magnificent teacher. You may often think of yourself as incapable, and yet all the while the answer you need is waiting in the wings.

Recognize that all that is worth thinking is available to you to harvest from the invisible environment around you. Understand that your physical, emotional, mental, and spiritual areas need constant quality attention. Without your positive input of energy-filled foods, electrically charged positive thoughts, and complete trust, along with surrender to God, all that you require to reach the Spirit will fall short.

We were given an opportunity to be the only creatures to know what our mission is, and we have become the only ones that have difficulty finding our mission. Each person has a unique and purposeful reason for being here. If we do not display this it is because we are foolishly wasting our time instead of devoting ourselves to the highest goal. Our actions are limited when our soul is not at the center of our pursuits.

***

Face yourself with the question "What is Truth?", and grow beyond the accepted ideas that we have surrounded it with, acknowledging that it is much more viable than anything we have ever perceived. Each day you are given freedom to synthesize more truth in your life. Truth is the

"Our actions are limited
when our soul is not at
the center of our pursuits."

baby looking up into the mother's eyes as the love is felt by all. That is a face of truth showing you the comfort of trust.

Enlightenment is acknowledging your own capacity to trust. Giving yourself constant support for all that you do will strengthen your integrity and enable you to do more, and to do better throughout your life. You can constantly access whatever you need through the development of trust. Do not question your motives and if you do, do not act.

When you have been hurt in the past it was only due to your failure to understand the whole reason for that occurrence. From your past you have created many reasons to doubt yourself. In your future you have every reason to fulfill your dreams. Like a volcano, a deep desire can gradually ignite you, to eventually pour your heart out on all that you do. Every successful person will tell you that they gave one hundred percent to reach their goal.

***

Each day as you look forward to your desired accomplishments, start by closing your eyes and saying a short prayer. It may sound something like this:

"Enlightenment is
acknowledgement
of your own capacity
to trust."

"Allow me today to have total confidence and trust, so that my integrity will lead me in the direction of truth. Give me the strength to stand strong and not be tempted to defend, but to accept, the wisdom to know when to contribute, and the awareness to know when to be silent."

The one minute it may take you to reflect on your coming actions may solidify a life of spirituality. Acknowledging positive action will give you the passion to proceed. Your instinct coupled with your passion will eternally ignite your possibilities.

From the communication you have with your own heart you can determine happiness or choose confusion. Cross messages only come to those who do not submit themselves to emotional discovery. Listen to yourself when speaking to your baby or pet. Your voice changes and you consciously permit elevating words to pour from you. Why is it that we do not always communicate with others so openly?

Harmony is a discovery process. It is not a formulated region of human experience. You will find this many times throughout your life when you permit awareness to guide you. Be consciously searching out the harmony that will encourage you to accept eternal life.

*"Harmony
is a discovery process."*

Conquor your fears by erasing them with knowledge. The limitations of fear are strengthened through your own sad convictions. They will melt away when you accept the glory of eternity. Your conversion is not necessary, but the committment of your heart and soul is. Wandering aimlessly without the knowledge that each breath is part of eternity disconnects us from the vibrant magic of acceptance. Go to the center of your thoughts to question their validity, and when you discover anything less than harmony discard those thoughts and aspire for greater.

***

Exist in a noble way without the arrogance of human normality. The abnormal is really the only thing that has moved humanity forward. The systemic normality that governs our every move prevents us from innovative and conscious progress.

When you begin your journey to God choose environments that are conducive to higher aspiration. Places of great peace and beauty, of holy structure and of nature will permit you to unwind and drink up the eternal wisdom in the moment.

Illuminate your pathway with the glowing experience of success, and reach further than your

*"Conquor your fears
by erasing them
with knowledge."*

own mind can imagine so that your goal is ever expanding. Freely pour out all of your hollow desires and replace them with your most spirited possibilities. Dream like a child, but act like a hero in pursuit of your aspirations.

Do not allow any practice to become routine. Order your life with definition and passion, accepting total responsibility for your choices and actions.

Be aware each day of the opportunities you are given to synthesize more truth in your life.

Acquire an abundance of happiness and freely share the overflow.

Know that your entire life is a mission of self-discovery, affirmation, accomplishment and release.

***

This book was written in the hope of expanding your idea of what spirituality can do for you. The message we want to share with you is that you are part of everything; you are always in the flow of eternity, and can be consciously aware of it when you choose to be. Take into your life those words that have sparked your desire in spirituality and let them blossom into fulfillment.

***

When accepting your own spirit
as a remarkable element in happiness,
you will feel among the blessed.
*Know that all healing in life
depends on it.*

HIPPOCRATES HEALTH INSTITUTE
1443 Palmdale Court
West Palm Beach, Florida 33411
(561) 471-8876

After 30 years in downtown Boston, the new home of Hippocrates Health Institute is on a beautiful tropical estate in West Palm Beach, Florida.

HIPPOCRATES HEALTH INSTITUTE

is well on its way to its 5th decade of helping people to help themselves back to a happy and healthy life. From every part of the globe guests arrive to participate in the Life-Change Program which gives them the practical tools to increase their spiritual, emotional and physical strength.

We hope to see you here someday soon!

(561) 471-8876

HEALTH EDUCATOR COURSE

Considered by many in the health field to be one of the most complete, state-of-the-art holistic health educations available anywhere, our Health Educator Course is designed to foster your career goals in the health field. The pace is fast and the instructors are demanding but the rewards more than compensate, enabling you to become a professional in the the physical, emotional, mental and spiritual aspects of holistic health.

Anatomy and physiology, counseling, science of living foods, structural alignment, polarity massage, fitness and exercise classes, organic gardening, colon health, electromagnetics, iridology, business and speaking skills, and live food preparation are some of the topics covered in the course.

The nine-week Health Educator Programs are offered every year. Contact us for complete details. (The length of the program, the dates, and the tuition may vary.)

Hippocrates Publications

by Brian and Anna Maria Clement

SPIRITUALITY
is the 6th book
in our 12 volume series entitled:

SERIES FOR LIVING

Read
LIVING FOODS FOR OPTIMUM HEALTH.

*A Highly Effective Program to Remove Toxins and
Restore Your Body to Vibrant Health.*

By Brian R. Clement
Foreword by Coretta Scott King.
(ISBN 0-7615-0258-0) 1996 $22.95
Prima Publishers

NOTES

NOTES

NOTES